# Organizational Management Theories

1st Edition

# Authors' Profile

**Muhammad Zeeshan Ali**
PMP, PMI-ACP

Enterprise Agile Coach | Trainer | Organizational Change Builder | Author | Certified Agile Practitioner

**Saqib Javed John**
PMP, PMI-ACP, ITIL

Author | Trainer | Certified Agile Practitioner | PMO | Organizational Development Consultant

Author of multiple books and numerous articles elaborating new dimensions of Agile framework and Traditional Project Management along with his work on Performance Management, PMO, Leadership, Team Building, and Personal Motivation. He is best known for designing the first of its kind "Performance Measurement Matrix" to calculate number-based performance indicators and scoring for both Software Engineering Individuals and Teams. Zeeshan is a great advocate and promoter of adaptation of Agile Methodologies, Processes, and Team Skill building.

Zeeshan has over 18 years' experience of managing 100+ mid-large scale, high visibility projects in both the Public and Private sectors. Experienced in managing several significant projects simultaneously and with a team spread over different geo-locations.

Zeeshan has Degrees in Project Management (MS) and Computer Sciences (BS). He has been certified as a Project Management Professional (PMP) and Agile Certified Professional (PMI-ACP) by Project Management Institute (PMI), USA.

Saqib is one of the founding members and Managing Director of Organizational Governance Management Consultants (OGMC). He has professional expertise of more than 18 years of working on enterprise projects in various business domains ranging from a functional organization to a projectized organization.

Saqib has immense experience in developing and managing human behavior, process engineering, and optimization, risk management, conflict management, performance maturity audits, and policy-making. This is one of the reasons he is relatable to readers of Business and management professions. He is best known for his rapid-learning techniques and easy methods of practical implementations. He also has contributed to many anthologies. His work is helping thousands of students, teachers, and professionals.

Saqib is MS (IT), certified "Project Management Professional" (PMP), and "Agile Certified Practitioner" (ACP) from Project Management Institute (PMI) U.S.A. He is also certified in "Information Technology Infrastructure Library" (ITIL) from Exin UK, "Sun Certified Java Programmer" (SCJP), and "Sun Certified Web Component Developer" (SCWCD) from Sun Microsystems USA.

Zeeshan and Saqib are also the Authors of **the Key Notes Series** which is gathering a lot of attention among the students, practitioners, and professionals of business and management sciences. All their publications can be reviewed at publications.ogmcs.com

Both actively publish their exclusive articles and their blog can be reached at blog.ogmcs.com

# Organizational Management
## Theories

1st Edition

**Muhammad Zeeshan Ali, PMP, PMI-ACP**

**Saqib Javed John, PMP, PMI-ACP, ITIL**

All inquiries should be addressed to (e-mail): info@ogmcpublications.com

First Printing: 2021

ISBN: 9798720062507

OGMC Publications

ogmcpublications.com

Ordering Information:
Special discounts are available on quantity purchases by corporations, associations, educators, and others. For details, contact the publisher at the above-listed address.

*Dedicated to all the readers*

*And*

*those who inspired this work.*

# Contents

# Preface

This book is a collection of exclusive theories put forward by the authors Muhammad Zeeshan Ali and Saqib Javed John. These theories are the essence of the experience they have gained, over the years working in multiple domains as well as methodologies.

These theories can be partially or fully implemented by organizations looking to improve the way their employees work. The important thing about these theories is that they are conceptualized not just keeping the top management in mind rather the scope extends from the top to the lowermost level.

In short, any professional with any level of experience can benefit from these theories despite the level at which he/she is working in the organization. Similarly, it is equally beneficial for those who are looking to start their own company and looking for a basis for the basic building blocks of the company.

This is the first edition and we will keep on adding more theories and concepts over time. As Authors and Professional Consultants, we will always be keen on listening to reader's feedback not just for improvements but also for potential new ideas and concepts.

# VISION

As discussed earlier, the framework can be either developed or adopted with some sort of modifications but the important thing to align it with the organization's vision, values, and strategy, etc. Keeping that in mind V.I.S.I.O.N (Ali & John, Private Life of Management, 2021) can be considered as the baseline in developing or adopting any framework.

V.I.S.I.O.N (Visualize, Identify, Structure, Implement, Operate, Nurture) is focused on providing the organizations and managers with dimensions to add to their original strategy and psychology.

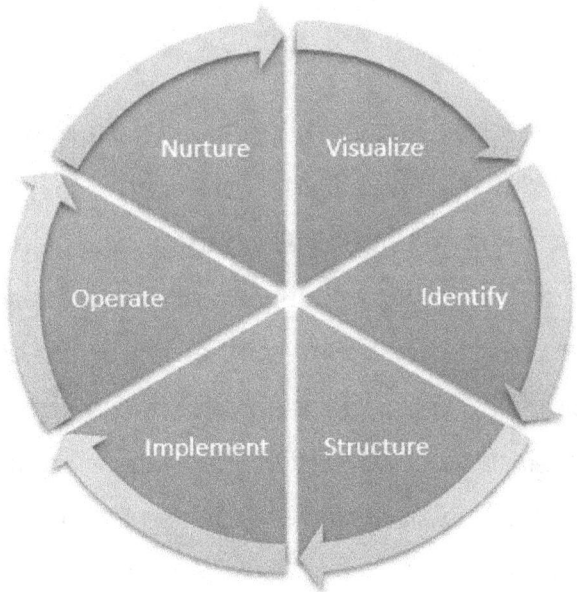

## V – Visualize:

It all starts with the visualization of the desired target. The very first question, in any planning framework, is "What?" or some cases "The Problem Statement". The output could be a product, service, result, or just a milestone but can be of any magnitude. Most of the time the vision is termed as being unrealistic but that is the case will everything that happened for the first time. If you cannot think big, then you cannot achieve it. Similarly, if you don't fail then you cannot learn anything. So the point is to your original vision because it will require commitment, motivation, and sacrifices which you cannot do when you try to peruse any other person's vision.

## I – Identify:

Once there is a clear target, then the next step is to determine the path to achieve that target. This is the part that is often termed as the "requirement Gathering and Understanding" phase. This step involved identifying all the pieces that will be required to achieve any target. Another important aspect of this step is to identify "when" an element will be required so it is procured right-in-time. This step involves the identification of not only the directly involved elements but also the ones that may be required indirectly.

## S – Structure:

The very next step is to formulate the strategy to put all the required pieces together. This is often the stage when some unidentified constraints are exposed and the whole framework has restart. Generally, around this phase, the potentially responsible persons and targeted dates for action points are identified and the whole translation of "how will things work" is defined in this phase.

## I – Implement:

Next is the time to put all planning into execution. In this step, the planned framework is implemented. The implementation can be done all across the organization at once or in phases. Similarly, the implementation can be limited to a certain group of people or areas before reviewing the results and deciding on the future strategy.

## O – Operate:

Once the framework is operational, next is to make the necessary adjustments to keep the framework aligned with the target. There might be some changes that may occur due to some technical or operational challenges and there will be others which the steering committee might be altered based on some results or response. The change can be in form of involvement of people at different stages based on their experience, skillset, and interests.

## N – Nurture:

This step is very important because any strategy or framework needs time to be effective and produce results. An Important thing to understand is that time is not required just for the framework to mature but also is required from the psychological aspect. The stakeholder sometimes has to be a bit extra patient to allow the framework to be fully functional. That is the way it is always recommended to give the framework some time before adjusting. The changes should be well thought out before their applications and once they are implemented, everybody has to be a bit patient to allow them time to take full effect.

# EDGE

The whole reason to go through the planning process is to gain an edge and for that, all the vital elements are categorized to form E.D.G.E. (Engagement, Directives, Goals, Excellence) (Ali & John, 2021)

## E – Engagement:

This element refers to the engagement of all the stakeholders and resources required to perform the assignment. Both the people you work with (Colleagues) and people you work for (Customer) are important as they directly affect all aspects of planning. The expertise, experience, and availability is often the most driving element in any planning.

Similarly, the level of domain knowledge, both for team and customer, is important in determining how much effort and time will be required to achieve the required level of understanding. This understanding could be at any stage of the project.

The same parameter is true for the other resources that need to be procured or made available during the project. The concept of "Just-in-Time" is important in the planning because early procurement will not be any good as the equipment will useless till the required time. It will not just require space and care but also may lose the warranty period. Another probability is that an upgraded version is released in the market while that old version is sitting in storage because it was procured well before the required timeline. Delay in acquiring resources has obvious consequences of affecting all timelines and all dependent tasks getting delay.

## D – Directives:

This element refers to the Laws, Processes, Frameworks, Procedures, Policies, and Protocols that encompass the project. Most of these sub-elements have their boundaries related to the domain and without following those, no kind of activities can proceed. The other thing about these sub-elements are they are generally defined by a third party and are aimed at keeping the competition fair.

As part of the planning team, the Directives are termed as unsupportive and unproductive, in most of the cases as they add overheads in terms of effort and thus taking more time to long complete the job without them. But the reality is that the benefits of having directives are durable and long-lasting but often they are realized after some time. That is the reason we, as consultants, always advise especially the senior management to be more patient and allow the adopted directives to mature before making a change.

Another important aspect of having these directives is to keep the playing field at the same level for all. That means equal opportunity for a newcomer as well as keeping the experienced persons or organizations at their toes. This brings in the "ever-improving" culture into individuals, teams, and organizations.

## G – Goals:

This element leads all the activities in a certain direction. As discussed earlier in other sections, there may be a combination of many motives towards setting a specific goal.

If you ask people, they will generally respond that the main goal for every individual or organization is to make money. That is true but if look into the success stories of individuals and organizations, we can see that they had some vision in mind for which they set themselves some goals, and to achieve that plan they had a roadmap.

That is the primary reason, having a roadmap is important because once that in place, next comes the activities to achieve the goals. Whatever challenges and hurdles come in the way, prove a life-time experience and adds some value. Commitment Determination and Perseverance are some of the aspects of human behavior that are tested throughout these challenges.

One thing that has always been the most common point of discussion is that the Goals should always be realistic. Try to achieve impossible only results in a waste of time and other resources. That is true to some effect but the other school-of-thought is that "you cannot achieve if you cannot dream". To achieve something, you got to have a vision and attitude to take the risks and face challenges.

I agree with the second school-of-thought. If you look at the people who made it to the top, their vision, especially at the start of the struggle, might have seemed impossible for the majority of people but once they were successful, they became role models for others. In the end, everybody tries to match their success but nobody talks about the failures and the hardships they faced leading up to that success.

What matters is not the number of times you have failed but how many times you were successful. Every time you failed, you learned something and you needed only one idea to be successful.

**E – Excellence:**

This element refers to consistently maintaining quality and consistently working towards improving it with each iteration.

This element binds all the other elements together and keeps on focusing on taking them to a next level.

Getting to your targets and achieving your goals is difficult but staying at the top level consistently is even more challenging. It is never easy to top something that is already at an exemplary level. Also, there are often concerns about having the risk of losing something that was making it so good.

The common practice to maintain and look for improvements is by having a dedicated effort in this regard. That is the reason organizations, around the world, now have a dedicated department that consistently monitors the activities and helps teams and individuals to achieve excellence. They also conduct frequent internal audits so that all the shortcomings are highlighted and can be then removed by working on them. This activity also prepares the organizations for external audits.

The external or independent audits are also aimed at reviewing the performance. The organizations now get certified through many Internationally Renowned Governing bodies. Clearing an audit and/or getting certified means that you as an individual or organization possess a verified and internationally recognized skillset.

The new growing trend, for organizations looking to excel, is to hire services of an independent consultant. As discussed in my other book (Ali & John, Inside Familiar Management, 2020), the consultant brings in experience from different domains and different sectors. Also, the experience of working with different clients, around the world, induces more dimensions to the regular work and they are much more familiar with cultural norms and jargons. Due to working with a large number of projects, they have been through a lot of different situations facing different and unique challenges which have helped them build a very good list of "Lesson Learned" regarding what to do and what not to do in such situations.

The good thing about consultants is that they possess knowledge and experience of practicing different methodologies and following different Industry best practices so they can implement processes that are suited to support the project based on the ground realities. The internal manager may lack this vision or might just be implementing a methodology or process just for the sake of company policy or his/her lack of knowledge.

Another good thing about engaging a consultant is that actually, you are hiring services not resources. It means that you get a team of experts to perform work rather than engaging a resource in the same manner as having the internal Project Manager. This aspect provides you with a lot of flexibility in terms of that you can add any services, as per need, whenever required and only for the required timeframe without increasing any head-count. Even in terms of cost, the services are "Pay-As-You-Go", which means that you pay for only services you used for only the duration of services.

One of the biggest differences and advantages I have noticed between hiring a consultant and an internal project manager is in the documentation related to the project. The consultants are much more skilled and comprehensive in preparing documentation. This is mainly due to the reason that there is a team of experts at the consultant's disposal that involves reviewing each piece of work at each phase. In the case of an internal Project Manager, this review is limited to a single person for most of the case and often proves a bottleneck and can overlook important information.

Apart from the skills aspect, hiring a consultant, the other important advantage is the psychological factor that comes in of having support in execution and decision making. No matter how much experience, the internal Project Manager has, he/she will always be influenced by company psychology and will always be inclined towards its employer. This results in often making Project Manager to "Sugar Coat" mainly to avoid displeasure from the top management. In the case of consultants, this "influence" is missing as they follow standard processes and practices. In my experience, this helps most in highlighting any risk or issue at its earliest stage and also keeping things transparent to all stakeholders.

# GROWTH

*"The Ultimate Management Psychology"*

Management is not just about processes, practices, and methodologies rather a large proportion of it purely depends on the emotional and behavioral psychology of the individuals as well as collectively as a team. Based on our professional experiences and learnings over the last two decades, we are introducing here a new concept of human resource development that is **"GROWTH".**

The basis of this concept "GROWTH" is that there is a set of different aspects of human behavior and psychology that can be fine-tuned to help professionals for rapid GROWTH and progress in their careers.

"GROWTH" is a combination of multiple behaviors (**G**overnance, **R**espect, **O**ptimism, **W**ellbeing, **T**eamwork, and **H**onesty) that combined to form the term "GROWTH" having the same meaning as the literary word Growth as per any English language dictionary.

Each element of growth is discussed as follows:

**Governance:**

The first element of "GROWTH" is Governance. It depicts that no matter what level you have achieved or which area you are working in, you always need guidance and expert support to grow as a professional. There is a famous phrase that "Learning Never Stops" and if you explore the term Governance, it will encapsulate a lot of things. A professional can seek Governance in terms of personal assistance from an expert or through the use of templates or any other piece of information. The key is that you always believe that you can always gain knowledge and support from anyone and at any time.

**Respect:**

Respect is a very important and fundamental part of human behavior which everyone seeks and it holds the key to real success. Respect is not just when the other person or party is right rather the best form of respect comes when the other person or party is at fault. Respect is an important part of communication because it makes you listen, absorb and then respond to the other party. Accepting your mistake is certainly a brave thing to do but accepting others is a level above that. Respect also means that you do not only acknowledge the experience of others but also their all skillset, hard work, and sacrifices behind that.

It is a universal fact that those who pay respect to others do earn the same in response.

**Optimism:**

Optimism is one of the personality characteristics which is mostly the main difference between success and failure. This attribute kept individuals focused on the positives even in a situation when everything is going wrong. A majority of professionals only present hope but if they don't have confidence then you are already a failure. There is a saying by William Arthur Ward that "If you can imagine it, you can achieve it. If you can dream it, you can become it." Once a professional build this mindset, he/she starts to look at things from a different perspective Optimism often leads to Perseverance and that mindset is important to excel beyond the common trough.

**Wellbeing:**

The personality of an individual is also defined by how he/she generally builds a perception of others. It is a quality of a great leader to think highly of others. Such leaders will always have a well-defined roadmap for others and will guide them every inch of the way to meet their targets. An important aspect of this characteristic is that when you think of the wellbeing of others, you will always use a positive frame of mind. Gradually this practice becomes a consistent part of your attitude and gradually turns into a habit and a work culture. It starts to benefit you in all aspects of your personal life as well. By thinking about the wellbeing of others, it starts introducing the act of sacrifice in your personality.

**Teamwork:**

Teamwork is all about developing trust among the team members, by ignoring their weaknesses and focusing on their strengths, and then gradually converging their weaknesses into strengths. When a group of people works together, the level of trust among them contributes towards their success. It's about building a relationship, over time, to an extent that you reach a point when you are making decisions based on not your but someone else's judgments. This is again a characteristic that elaborates positivity in your personality. You take others along in making decisions and get benefits or penalized from that. The thing you learn through trust is understanding and realizing the fact that it is not always about you. You have to build a professional relationship to achieve that added advantage and grow in your career.

**Honesty:**

This is also a very important aspect of human behavior and conduct. As soon as you honestly accept your mistake, that is the time to start mitigating the faults and grow as a true professional. Accepting mistakes is never easy especially when someone else shares your shortcomings but the people around you will combine their efforts to take care of the issue created by you.

Another aspect about being honest is that you recognize and rectify if there is any gap in your skillset or personality thus indicating your readiness to learn to overcome that gap. Honesty again is the source of elaborating positivity, as you accept, you need others. For honest decisions, you get to use the highest level of your skills and as a result, start challenging yourself to deliver more.

# GROWTH

---

# REACH

The purpose and phenomena behind the R.E.A.C.H are to build a Progressively Elaborated Process to implement the BASICS of Project Management irrespective of any particular framework or methodology.

REACH is a "Strategic Iterative Process", execute in a loop to provide maximum output. The design of this process is very lean, efficient, and productive.

**Realize...** the problem

**Evolve...** through Re-engineering of processes or by changing the methodology

**Adapt...** new designs, innovation, and changes to transform

**Convert...** all positive and productive changes into policies and standard operating procedures (SOPs) to improve the working culture of an organization

History…  archive lesson learned and analytics for the future validations and negotiations (also known as Organizational Process Assets)

---

**Realize:**

Realization is the first and fundamental element of the REACH concept as its well-known truth in the project management that "OGMC – Projects never work on assumption or uncertainties"

In any Project, framework, or execution method, the more we identify what is useless and irrelevant, the better would be planning, execution and delivery. Project deliveries should be exactly as per the agreed scope neither under-promise and nor above the commitments. In both cases, it will be a failure.

After identifying and realizing the irrelevant elements in requirements and scope, we recommend "Avoid", which is one of the Risk Response Strategies, as the best solution to minimize the risks that can be caused in the result.

Along with the scope of work, management also needs to identify and avoid the waste of time on the over follow-ups with the teams and Teams should not waste time on the over treatments of the issues or bugs. This element shifts focus to identify what is exactly required' and 'what is important.

Our expert opinion on realization is that "Eliminate unnecessary factors and cultivate essentials"

**Evolve:**

Evolution is the 2nd element of the REACH concept also well-known as Continuous Improvement in both functional and projectized work environment, "OGMC – Move, to know the Hurdles".

Evolution is the result of Mindset and Approach but not only of the leaders and experts but beyond it's about the mindset of the whole organization that makes a real difference. Ideas should drive the strategies and then strategies should drive the work culture of an organization, not the otherwise

In Project Management, rapid developments in technology, frameworks, and execution methodologies are the best example of evolution. Keep validating and keep changing the methods until you achieve the desired results in form of improved workflows or optimized processes.

## Adapt:

Adaptability is the 3rd and central-main element of the REACH concept, *"OGMC – the Most Adaptive Processes are the Fittest"*

The biggest challenge and distraction in any organization or project is the change resistance, which executives, management, and even teams within themselves face most of the time. We normally face such hurdles in our work environments that affect adaptability.

Adaptability by the evolutionary improvements is required to be treated as an essential part of the work culture and processes improvements. It is about the readiness and flexibility to adapt to the changes in system, approach, processes, and work conditions. Always remains flexible to negotiate for the betterment and improvement.

## Convert:

Conversion is the 4th (i.e. 2nd last) element of the REACH concept, "OGMC – Conversion is the Master Act". In any business, organization or project, constructive conversion and transformation is the most important daily factor to grow together. In this part of the process, it's time to convert the best processes, plans, and methods into long-term policies and

SOPs. This is a stage where the finest and the most effective form of the process becomes the benchmark for the upcoming projects within the organization as well as on global platforms.

Process conversion into policy depends on the right delivery and result of the process. Speed of Conversion affects the speed of business and productivity.

**History:**

History is the last element of the REACH concept, *"OGMC – No History, No Learning"*

This is knowledge management or building Organization Process Assets.

Knowledge Archives for any project or program or portfolio are as important as Enterprise Environmental Factors are. This is the factor that makes organizations independent and discourages people dependency. As it contains the best and proven rules, analytics, checklists, lessons learned, and parameters.

Lessons from past projects and statements of efficient executions play a huge contribution in decision making and setting the right approach and strategy for future projects. Apart from individual new learning, I firmly believe in Learning in Collaboration, through the History or Archives.

# References

Ali, M. Z., & John, S. J. (2020). *Inside Familiar Management.* OGMC Publications.

Ali, M. Z., & John, S. J. (2021). *Applied Psychosomatic Planning.* OGMC Publications.

Ali, M. Z., & John, S. J. (2021). *Private Life of Management.* OGMC Publications.

# References

www.ingramcontent.com/pod-product-compliance
Lightning Source LLC
Chambersburg PA
CBHW071123220526
45467CB00004B/2035